Name

Address

I0139623

Telephone

Email

Club/School   Membership No.

Diving Qualifications

DIVED UP

Log Book No.

ISBN 978-1-909455-07-8

Printed by Lightning Source.

Published 2013 by
Dived Up Publications
Oxford, United Kingdom
Email info@divedup.com
Web www.DivedUp.com

DIVED UP

FIT FOR UNDERWATER EXPLORING

YOUR
DIVE LOGS

DIVE LOG

DIVE No.

Date

Dive Site

Boat/Shore/Inland

Buddy

Purpose

Boat/Skipper

Port/Launch Site

Dive of Day   1   2   3   4   Surface Int.   :   Time in   :   out   :

Mix	Pressure		Used	Cyl. Size
	In	Out		

DIVE TIME

mins

MAX DEPTH

m/ft

Tissue Code: Pre   Post   Deco Stops .... mins .... m/ft .... mins .... m/ft

Open Circuit ☐   Semi-Closed ☐   Closed Circuit ☐   Comp/Tables ....

Weight ....kg/lbs   OK: Y / N   (Add/Remove ....)

Suit/Undersuit ....Gloves Y / N   Hood Y / N   Hot / Cold / OK

Water Speed   Slack / Slow / Steady / Fast   Temp @ Depth

Sea State   Wind Speed   Temp @ Surface

0

Depth

Time   5   10   15   20   25   30   35   40   45   50   55   60   65   70   75   80   85   90   95   100

Summary

Vis & Water Colour

m/ft

1	
2	
3	
4	
5	
6	
7	
8	
9	
10	
11	
12	
13	
14	
15	
16	
17	
18	
19	
20	
21	
22	
23	
24	
25	

Description/Sketch

DIVED UP

Accumulated Dive Time

:

Milestone

Name

Signature

No.

Verified by

DIVE No.	**DIVE LOG**	Date

Dive Site   Boat/Shore/Inland

Buddy   Purpose

Boat/Skipper   Port/Launch Site

Dive of Day   1   2   3   4   Surface Int.   :   Time in   :   out   :

		Pressure				
Mix	In	Out	Used	Cyl. Size		

DIVE TIME

mins

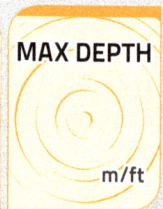

MAX DEPTH

m/ft

Tissue Code: Pre   Post   Deco Stops .... mins .... m/ft   ....mins........ m/ft

Open Circuit ☐   Semi-Closed ☐   Closed Circuit ☐   Comp/Tables ....

Weight ....kg/lbs   OK: Y / N   (Add/Remove ....)

Suit/Undersuit ....Gloves Y / N   Hood Y / N   Hot / Cold / OK

Water Speed   Slack / Slow / Steady / Fast   Temp @ Depth

Sea State   Wind Speed   Temp @ Surface

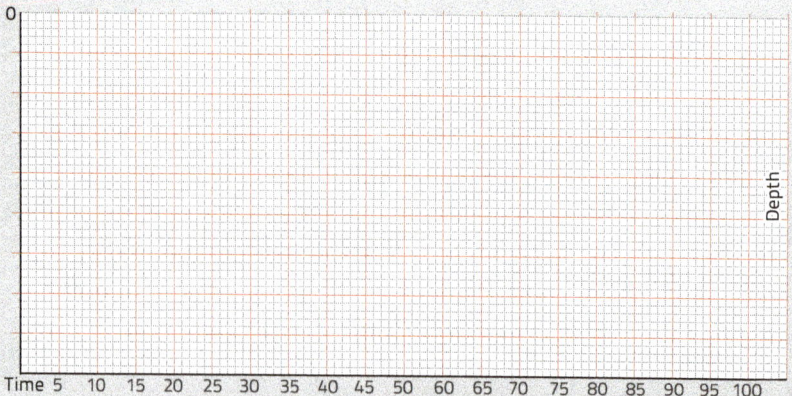

Summary

	1
	2
	3
	4
	5
	6
	7
	8
	9
	10
	11
	12
	13
	14
	15
	16
	17
	18
	19
	20
	21
	22
	23
	24
	25

Description/Sketch

DIVED UP

Accumulated Dive Time

:

Milestone

Name

Signature

No.

Verified by

DIVE LOG

DIVE No.

Date

Dive Site	Boat/Shore/Inland
Buddy	Purpose
Boat/Skipper	Port/Launch Site

Dive of Day 1 2 3 4   Surface Int.   :   Time in   :   out   :

	Pressure			
Mix	In	Out	Used	Cyl. Size

DIVE TIME

mins

MAX DEPTH

m/ft

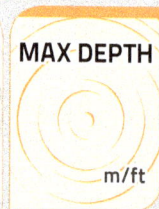

Tissue Code: Pre   Post   Deco Stops .... mins .... m/ft   .... mins........ m/ft

Open Circuit [ ]   Semi-Closed [ ]   Closed Circuit [ ]   Comp/Tables ....

Weight ....kg/lbs   OK: Y / N   (Add/Remove ....)

Suit/Undersuit ....Gloves Y / N   Hood Y / N   Hot / Cold / OK

Water Speed   Slack / Slow / Steady / Fast   Temp @ Depth

Sea State   Wind Speed   Temp @ Surface

0

Depth

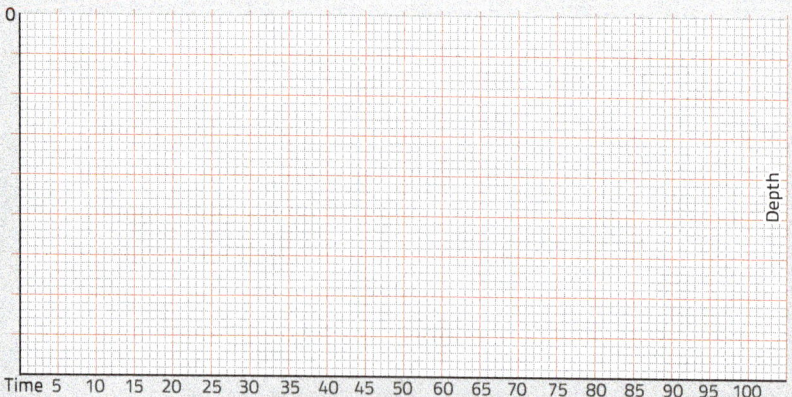

Time 5 10 15 20 25 30 35 40 45 50 55 60 65 70 75 80 85 90 95 100

Summary

Description/Sketch

Vis & Water Colour

m/ft

1	
2	
3	
4	
5	
6	
7	
8	
9	
10	
11	
12	
13	
14	
15	
16	
17	
18	
19	
20	
21	
22	
23	
24	
25	

Accumulated Dive Time

:

Milestone

Name

Signature

No.

Verified by

DIVE No.	**DIVE LOG**	Date

Dive Site
Boat/Shore/Inland

Buddy
Purpose

Boat/Skipper
Port/Launch Site

Dive of Day 1 2 3 4   Surface Int.   :   Time in   :   out   :

		Pressure				
Mix	In	Out	Used	Cyl. Size		

DIVE TIME mins

MAX DEPTH m/ft

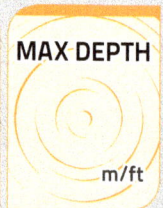

Tissue Code: Pre   Post   Deco Stops .... mins .... m/ft ....mins ....m/ft

Open Circuit ☐   Semi-Closed ☐   Closed Circuit ☐   Comp/Tables ....

Weight ....kg/lbs   OK: Y / N   (Add/Remove ....)

Suit/Undersuit ....Gloves Y / N   Hood Y / N   Hot / Cold / OK

Water Speed Slack / Slow / Steady / Fast   Temp @ Depth

Sea State   Wind Speed   Temp @ Surface

0

Depth

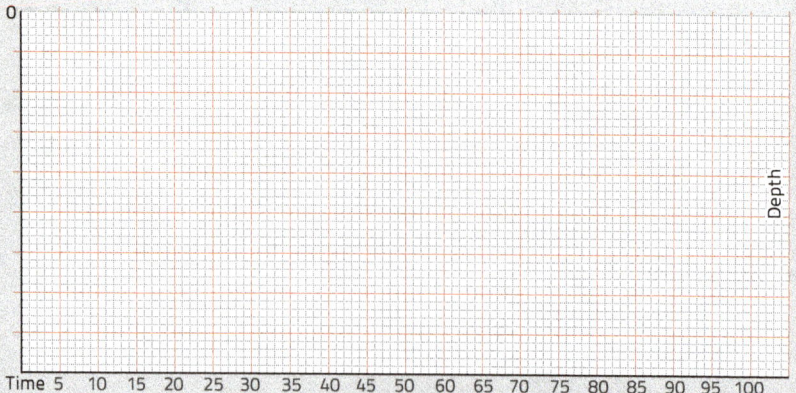

Time 5 10 15 20 25 30 35 40 45 50 55 60 65 70 75 80 85 90 95 100

Summary

Vis & Water Colour

m/ft

1	
2	
3	
4	
5	
6	
7	
8	
9	
10	
11	
12	
13	
14	
15	
16	
17	
18	
19	
20	
21	
22	
23	
24	
25	

Description/Sketch

DIVED UP

Accumulated Dive Time

:

Milestone

Name

Signature

No.

Verified by

DIVE LOG

DIVE No.

Date

Dive Site

Boat/Shore/Inland

Buddy

Purpose

Boat/Skipper

Port/Launch Site

Dive of Day   1   2   3   4   Surface Int.   :   Time in   :   out   :

Mix	Pressure		Used	Cyl. Size
	In	Out		

DIVE TIME

mins

MAX DEPTH

m/ft

Tissue Code: Pre   Post   Deco Stops .... mins .... m/ft   .... mins .... m/ft

Open Circuit ☐   Semi-Closed ☐   Closed Circuit ☐   Comp/Tables ....

Weight ....kg/lbs   OK: Y / N   (Add/Remove ....)

Suit/Undersuit ....Gloves Y / N   Hood Y / N   Hot / Cold / OK

Water Speed   Slack / Slow / Steady / Fast   Temp @ Depth

Sea State   Wind Speed   Temp @ Surface

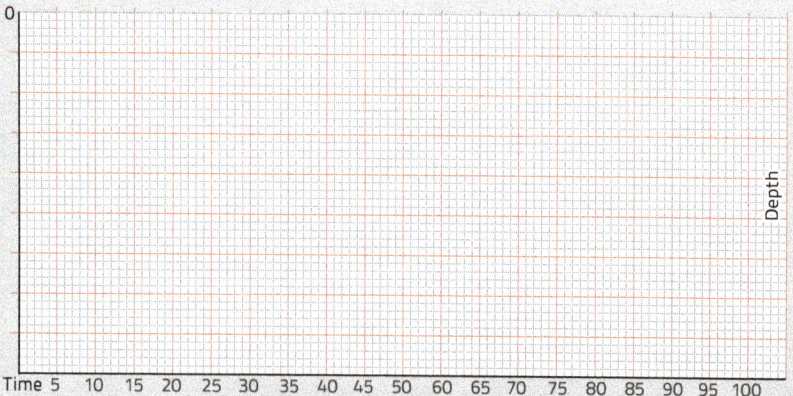

Time   5   10   15   20   25   30   35   40   45   50   55   60   65   70   75   80   85   90   95   100

Depth

Summary

Vis & Water Colour

m/ft

1	
2	
3	
4	
5	
6	
7	
8	
9	
10	
11	
12	
13	
14	
15	
16	
17	
18	
19	
20	
21	
22	
23	
24	
25	

Description/Sketch

DIVED UP

Accumulated Dive Time

:

Milestone

Name

Signature

No.

Verified by

DIVE LOG

DIVE No.		Date

Dive Site 　　　　　　　Boat/Shore/Inland

Buddy 　　　　　　　Purpose

Boat/Skipper 　　　　　　　Port/Launch Site

Dive of Day　1　2　3　4　　Surface Int.　　:　　Time in　　:　　out　　:

Mix	In	Pressure Out	Used	Cyl. Size

DIVE TIME

mins

MAX DEPTH

m/ft

Tissue Code: Pre　　Post　　Deco Stops …… mins …… m/ft ……mins……m/ft

Open Circuit ☐　Semi-Closed ☐　Closed Circuit ☐　Comp/Tables …………………………
Weight ………………kg/lbs　OK: Y / N　(Add/Remove ………………)
Suit/Undersuit ………………………………………Gloves Y / N　Hood Y / N　Hot / Cold / OK

Water Speed　Slack / Slow / Steady / Fast　　　Temp @ Depth
Sea State　　　　　Wind Speed　　　　Temp @ Surface

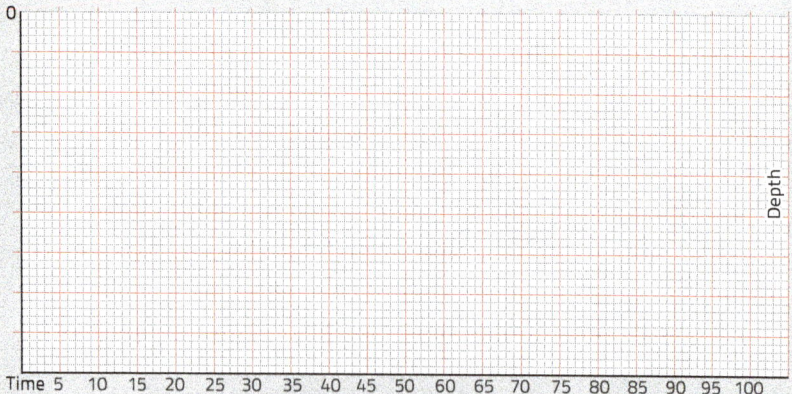

0

Depth

Time 5　10　15　20　25　30　35　40　45　50　55　60　65　70　75　80　85　90　95　100

Summary

Description/Sketch

Vis & Water Colour

m/ft

1	
2	
3	
4	
5	
6	
7	
8	
9	
10	
11	
12	
13	
14	
15	
16	
17	
18	
19	
20	
21	
22	
23	
24	
25	

Accumulated Dive Time

:

Milestone

Name

Signature

No.

Verified by

| DIVE No. | **DIVE LOG** | Date |

Dive Site   Boat/Shore/Inland

Buddy   Purpose

Boat/Skipper   Port/Launch Site

Dive of Day 1 2 3 4 | Surface Int.   : | Time in   :   out   :

	Pressure			
Mix	In	Out	Used	Cyl. Size

DIVE TIME

mins

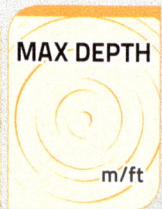

MAX DEPTH

m/ft

Tissue Code: Pre   Post | Deco Stops .... mins .... m/ft   ....mins .... m/ft

Open Circuit ☐   Semi-Closed ☐   Closed Circuit ☐   Comp/Tables ....

Weight ....kg/lbs   OK: Y / N   (Add/Remove ....)

Suit/Undersuit ....Gloves Y / N   Hood Y / N   Hot / Cold / OK

Water Speed Slack / Slow / Steady / Fast   Temp @ Depth

Sea State   Wind Speed   Temp @ Surface

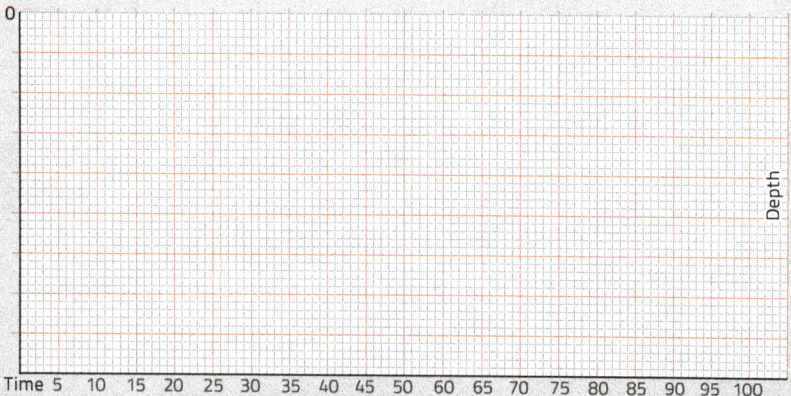

0

Depth

Time 5   10   15   20   25   30   35   40   45   50   55   60   65   70   75   80   85   90   95   100

Summary

Vis & Water Colour

m/ft

Description/Sketch

1
2
3
4
5
6
7
8
9
10
11
12
13
14
15
16
17
18
19
20
21
22
23
24
25

DIVED UP

Accumulated Dive Time	Name	Verified by
:	Signature	
Milestone	No.	

DIVE LOG

DIVE No.

Date

Dive Site	Boat/Shore/Inland
Buddy	Purpose
Boat/Skipper	Port/Launch Site

Dive of Day 1 2 3 4   Surface Int.   :   Time in   :   out   :

Mix	Pressure		Used	Cyl. Size
	In	Out		

DIVE TIME

mins

MAX DEPTH

m/ft

Tissue Code: Pre   Post   Deco Stops .... mins .... m/ft .... mins .... m/ft

Open Circuit ☐   Semi-Closed ☐   Closed Circuit ☐   Comp/Tables ....

Weight .... kg/lbs   OK: Y / N   (Add/Remove ....)

Suit/Undersuit .... Gloves Y / N   Hood Y / N   Hot / Cold / OK

Water Speed Slack / Slow / Steady / Fast   Temp @ Depth

Sea State   Wind Speed   Temp @ Surface

0

Depth

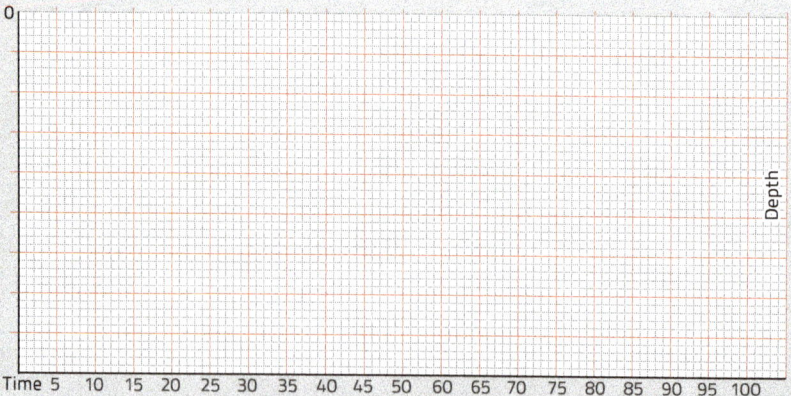

Time 5   10   15   20   25   30   35   40   45   50   55   60   65   70   75   80   85   90   95   100

Summary

m/ft

Description/Sketch

DIVED UP

	1
	2
	3
	4
	5
	6
	7
	8
	9
	10
	11
	12
	13
	14
	15
	16
	17
	18
	19
	20
	21
	22
	23
	24
	25

Accumulated Dive Time	Name	Verified by
:	Signature	
Milestone	No.	

DIVE No.	DIVE LOG	Date

Dive Site   Boat/Shore/Inland

Buddy   Purpose

Boat/Skipper   Port/Launch Site

Dive of Day   1   2   3   4   Surface Int.   :   Time in   :   out   :

	Pressure				DIVE TIME	MAX DEPTH
Mix	In	Out	Used	Cyl. Size		

DIVE TIME   mins

MAX DEPTH   m/ft

Tissue Code: Pre   Post   Deco Stops .... mins .... m/ft .... mins .... m/ft

Open Circuit ☐   Semi-Closed ☐   Closed Circuit ☐   Comp/Tables ....

Weight .... kg/lbs   OK: Y / N   (Add/Remove ....)

Suit/Undersuit ....Gloves Y / N   Hood Y / N   Hot / Cold / OK

Water Speed   Slack / Slow / Steady / Fast   Temp @ Depth

Sea State   Wind Speed   Temp @ Surface

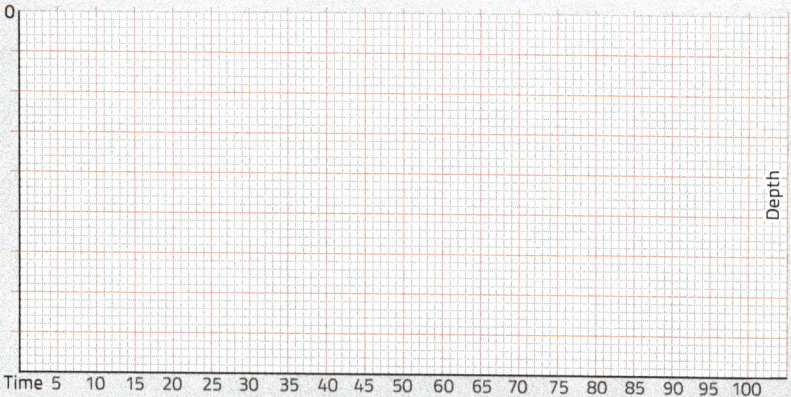

Time 5   10   15   20   25   30   35   40   45   50   55   60   65   70   75   80   85   90   95   100

Depth

Summary

Description/Sketch

Vis & Water Colour

m/ft

1
2
3
4
5
6
7
8
9
10
11
12
13
14
15
16
17
18
19
20
21
22
23
24
25

Accumulated Dive Time

:

Milestone

Name

Signature

No.

Verified by

DIVE No.	**DIVE LOG**	Date

Dive Site Boat/Shore/Inland

Buddy Purpose

Boat/Skipper Port/Launch Site

Dive of Day 1 2 3 4   Surface Int.   :   Time in   :   out   :

		Pressure				
Mix	In	Out	Used	Cyl. Size		

DIVE TIME

mins

MAX DEPTH

m/ft

Tissue Code: Pre   Post   Deco Stops .... mins .... m/ft   .... mins .... m/ft

Open Circuit ☐   Semi-Closed ☐   Closed Circuit ☐   Comp/Tables ....

Weight .... kg/lbs   OK: Y / N   (Add/Remove ....)

Suit/Undersuit .... Gloves Y / N   Hood Y / N   Hot / Cold / OK

Water Speed Slack / Slow / Steady / Fast   Temp @ Depth

Sea State   Wind Speed   Temp @ Surface

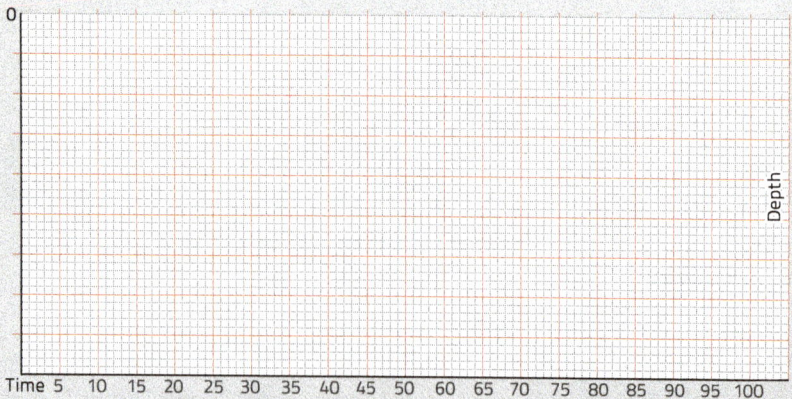

Summary

Description/Sketch

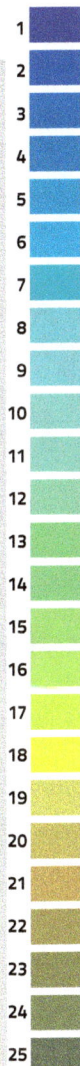

Vis & Water Colour

m/ft

1
2
3
4
5
6
7
8
9
10
11
12
13
14
15
16
17
18
19
20
21
22
23
24
25

DIVED UP

Accumulated Dive Time
:
Milestone

Name

Signature

No.

Verified by

DIVE LOG

DIVE No.

Date

Dive Site

Boat/Shore/Inland

Buddy

Purpose

Boat/Skipper

Port/Launch Site

Dive of Day   1   2   3   4   Surface Int.   :   Time in   :   out   :

Mix	Pressure		Used	Cyl. Size
	In	Out		

DIVE TIME

mins

MAX DEPTH

m/ft

Tissue Code: Pre   Post   Deco Stops .... mins .... m/ft   ....mins........ m/ft

Open Circuit ☐   Semi-Closed ☐   Closed Circuit ☐   Comp/Tables ....

Weight ....kg/lbs   OK: Y / N   (Add/Remove ....)

Suit/Undersuit ....Gloves Y / N   Hood Y / N   Hot / Cold / OK

Water Speed   Slack / Slow / Steady / Fast   Temp @ Depth

Sea State   Wind Speed   Temp @ Surface

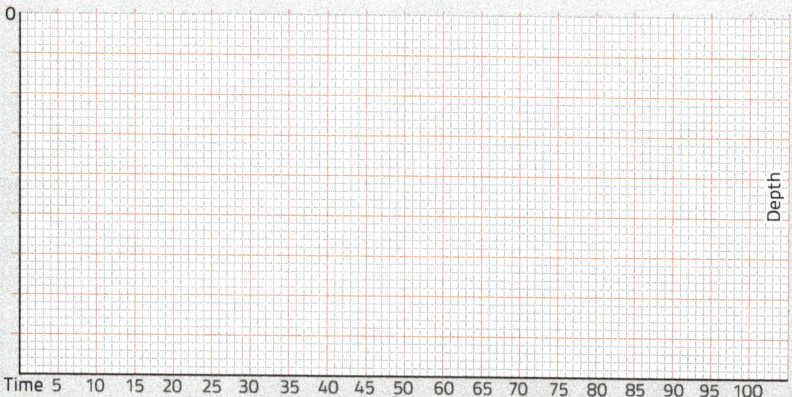

Depth

Time 5   10   15   20   25   30   35   40   45   50   55   60   65   70   75   80   85   90   95   100

Summary

Description/Sketch

DIVED UP

Vis & Water Colour

m/ft

1	
2	
3	
4	
5	
6	
7	
8	
9	
10	
11	
12	
13	
14	
15	
16	
17	
18	
19	
20	
21	
22	
23	
24	
25	

Accumulated Dive Time

:

Milestone

Name

Signature

No.

Verified by

DIVE No.	**DIVE LOG**	Date

Dive Site ___ Boat/Shore/Inland

Buddy ___ Purpose

Boat/Skipper ___ Port/Launch Site

Dive of Day 1 2 3 4   Surface Int.   :   Time in   :   out   :

	Pressure			
Mix	In	Out	Used	Cyl. Size

DIVE TIME ___ mins

MAX DEPTH ___ m/ft

Tissue Code: Pre   Post   Deco Stops .... mins .... m/ft .... mins .... m/ft

Open Circuit ☐   Semi-Closed ☐   Closed Circuit ☐   Comp/Tables ....

Weight ....kg/lbs   OK: Y / N   (Add/Remove ....)

Suit/Undersuit ....Gloves Y / N   Hood Y / N   Hot / Cold / OK

Water Speed Slack / Slow / Steady / Fast   Temp @ Depth

Sea State   Wind Speed   Temp @ Surface

0

Depth

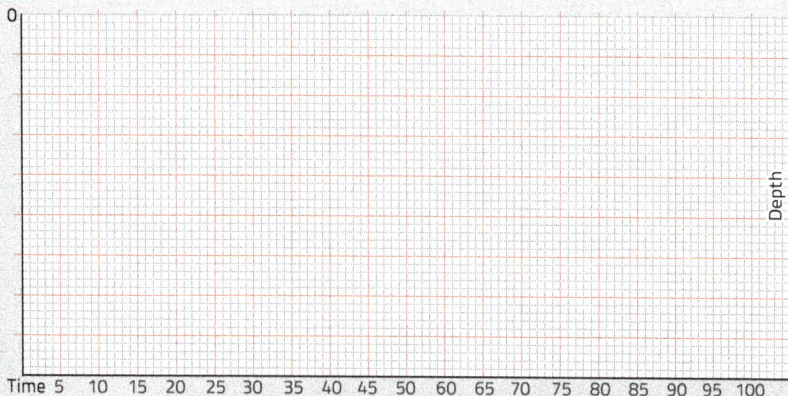

Time 5 10 15 20 25 30 35 40 45 50 55 60 65 70 75 80 85 90 95 100

Summary

Description/Sketch

Vis & Water Colour

m/ft

1	
2	
3	
4	
5	
6	
7	
8	
9	
10	
11	
12	
13	
14	
15	
16	
17	
18	
19	
20	
21	
22	
23	
24	
25	

DIVED UP

Accumulated Dive Time	Name	Verified by
:	Signature	
Milestone	No.	

DIVE No.	DIVE LOG	Date

Dive Site   Boat/Shore/Inland

Buddy   Purpose

Boat/Skipper   Port/Launch Site

Dive of Day   1   2   3   4   Surface Int.   :   Time in   :   out   :

	Pressure					
Mix	In	Out	Used	Cyl. Size	**DIVE TIME**	**MAX DEPTH**
					mins	m/ft

Tissue Code: Pre   Post   Deco Stops .... mins .... m/ft   ....mins........ m/ft

Open Circuit ☐   Semi-Closed ☐   Closed Circuit ☐   Comp/Tables ....

Weight ....kg/lbs   OK: Y / N   (Add/Remove ....)

Suit/Undersuit ....Gloves Y / N   Hood Y / N   Hot / Cold / OK

Water Speed   Slack / Slow / Steady / Fast   Temp @ Depth

Sea State   Wind Speed   Temp @ Surface

Time 5   10   15   20   25   30   35   40   45   50   55   60   65   70   75   80   85   90   95   100

Depth

Summary

Description/Sketch

Vis & Water Colour

m/ft

1	
2	
3	
4	
5	
6	
7	
8	
9	
10	
11	
12	
13	
14	
15	
16	
17	
18	
19	
20	
21	
22	
23	
24	
25	

DIVED UP

Accumulated Dive Time

:

Milestone

Name

Signature

No.

Verified by

DIVE LOG

DIVE No.

Date

Dive Site   Boat/Shore/Inland

Buddy   Purpose

Boat/Skipper   Port/Launch Site

Dive of Day   1   2   3   4   Surface Int.   :   Time in   :   out   :

| Mix | Pressure | | Used | Cyl. Size |
	In	Out		

DIVE TIME

mins

MAX DEPTH

m/ft

Tissue Code: Pre   Post   Deco Stops .... mins .... m/ft .... mins .... m/ft

Open Circuit ☐   Semi-Closed ☐   Closed Circuit ☐   Comp/Tables ....
Weight .... kg/lbs   OK: Y / N   (Add/Remove ....)
Suit/Undersuit ....Gloves Y / N   Hood Y / N   Hot / Cold / OK

Water Speed   Slack / Slow / Steady / Fast   Temp @ Depth
Sea State   Wind Speed   Temp @ Surface

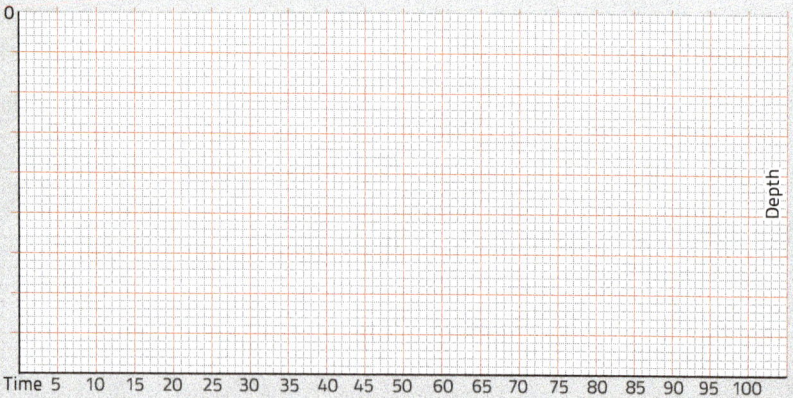

Time 5   10   15   20   25   30   35   40   45   50   55   60   65   70   75   80   85   90   95   100

Summary

Description/Sketch

1	
2	
3	
4	
5	
6	
7	
8	
9	
10	
11	
12	
13	
14	
15	
16	
17	
18	
19	
20	
21	
22	
23	
24	
25	

DIVED UP

Accumulated Dive Time

:

Milestone

Name

Signature

No.

Verified by

DIVE LOG

DIVE No.

Date

| Dive Site | Boat/Shore/Inland |

Buddy — Purpose

Boat/Skipper — Port/Launch Site

Dive of Day 1 2 3 4   Surface Int.   :   Time in   :   out   :

| | Pressure | | | | DIVE TIME | MAX DEPTH |
| Mix | In | Out | Used | Cyl. Size | | |

mins   m/ft

Tissue Code: Pre   Post   Deco Stops .... mins .... m/ft .... mins .... m/ft

Open Circuit ☐   Semi-Closed ☐   Closed Circuit ☐   Comp/Tables ....

Weight .... kg/lbs   OK: Y / N   (Add/Remove ....)

Suit/Undersuit .... Gloves Y / N   Hood Y / N   Hot / Cold / OK

Water Speed Slack / Slow / Steady / Fast   Temp @ Depth

Sea State   Wind Speed   Temp @ Surface

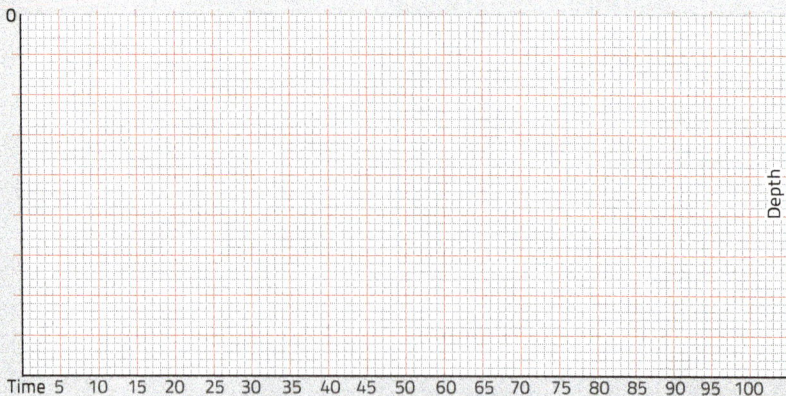

0

Depth

Time 5 10 15 20 25 30 35 40 45 50 55 60 65 70 75 80 85 90 95 100

Summary

Description/Sketch

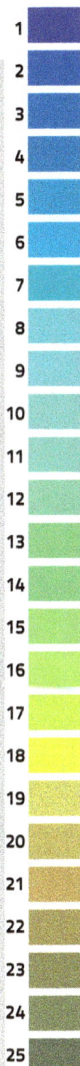

Vis & Water Colour

m/ft

1
2
3
4
5
6
7
8
9
10
11
12
13
14
15
16
17
18
19
20
21
22
23
24
25

DIVED UP

Accumulated Dive Time	Name	Verified by
:	Signature	
Milestone	No.	

DIVE No.	**DIVE LOG**	Date

Dive Site — Boat/Shore/Inland

Buddy — Purpose

Boat/Skipper — Port/Launch Site

Dive of Day 1 2 3 4 | Surface Int. : | Time in :   out :

	Pressure				DIVE TIME	MAX DEPTH
Mix	In	Out	Used	Cyl. Size		

DIVE TIME .... mins

MAX DEPTH .... m/ft

Tissue Code: Pre   Post | Deco Stops .... mins .... m/ft ....mins .... m/ft

Open Circuit ☐   Semi-Closed ☐   Closed Circuit ☐   Comp/Tables ....

Weight .... kg/lbs   OK: Y / N   (Add/Remove ....)

Suit/Undersuit ....Gloves Y / N   Hood Y / N   Hot / Cold / OK

Water Speed Slack / Slow / Steady / Fast   Temp @ Depth

Sea State   Wind Speed   Temp @ Surface

Summary

Description/Sketch

1
2
3
4
5
6
7
8
9
10
11
12
13
14
15
16
17
18
19
20
21
22
23
24
25

DIVED UP

Accumulated Dive Time	Name	Verified by
:	Signature	
Milestone	No.	

DIVE No.	DIVE LOG	Date

Dive Site   Boat/Shore/Inland

Buddy   Purpose

Boat/Skipper   Port/Launch Site

Dive of Day   1   2   3   4   Surface Int.   :   Time in   :   out   :

Mix	Pressure		Used	Cyl. Size	DIVE TIME	MAX DEPTH
	In	Out				
					mins	m/ft

Tissue Code: Pre   Post   Deco Stops .... mins .... m/ft ....mins........ m/ft

Open Circuit ☐   Semi-Closed ☐   Closed Circuit ☐   Comp/Tables ....

Weight .... kg/lbs   OK: Y / N   (Add/Remove ....)

Suit/Undersuit ....Gloves Y / N   Hood Y / N   Hot / Cold / OK

Water Speed   Slack / Slow / Steady / Fast   Temp @ Depth

Sea State   Wind Speed   Temp @ Surface

0

Depth

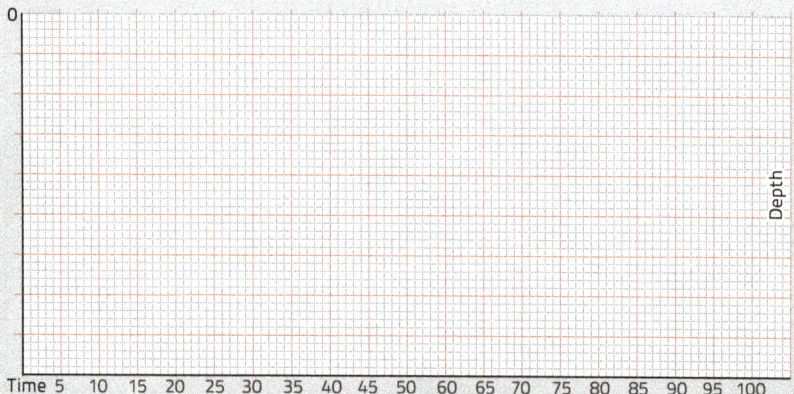

Time   5   10   15   20   25   30   35   40   45   50   55   60   65   70   75   80   85   90   95   100

Summary

Vis & Water Colour

m/ft

1
2
3
4
5
6
7
8
9
10
11
12
13
14
15
16
17
18
19
20
21
22
23
24
25

Description/Sketch

DIVED UP

Accumulated Dive Time	Name	Verified by
:	Signature	
Milestone	No.	

DIVE No.	DIVE LOG	Date

Dive Site | Boat/Shore/Inland

Buddy | Purpose

Boat/Skipper | Port/Launch Site

Dive of Day 1 2 3 4 | Surface Int.   : | Time in   :   out   :

Mix	Pressure In	Out	Used	Cyl. Size	DIVE TIME	MAX DEPTH
					mins	m/ft

Tissue Code: Pre   Post | Deco Stops .... mins .... m/ft .... mins .... m/ft

Open Circuit ☐ Semi-Closed ☐ Closed Circuit ☐ Comp/Tables ....

Weight ....kg/lbs   OK: Y / N   (Add/Remove ....)

Suit/Undersuit ....Gloves Y / N   Hood Y / N   Hot / Cold / OK

Water Speed Slack / Slow / Steady / Fast | Temp @ Depth

Sea State | Wind Speed | Temp @ Surface

0

Depth

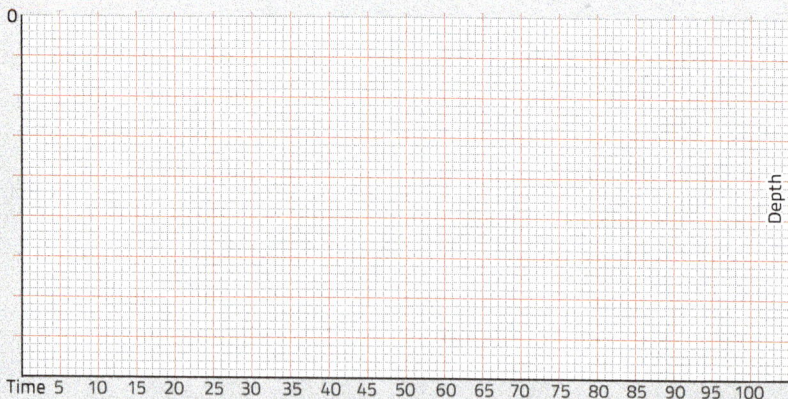

Time 5 10 15 20 25 30 35 40 45 50 55 60 65 70 75 80 85 90 95 100

Summary

Description/Sketch

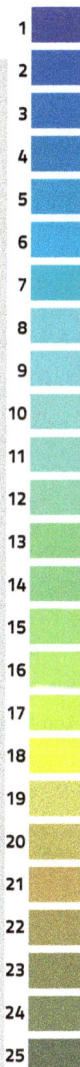

Vis & Water Colour

m/ft

1
2
3
4
5
6
7
8
9
10
11
12
13
14
15
16
17
18
19
20
21
22
23
24
25

DIVED UP

Accumulated Dive Time		Verified by
:	Name	
Milestone	Signature	
	No.	

DIVE No.	**DIVE LOG**	Date

Dive Site | Boat/Shore/Inland

Buddy | Purpose

Boat/Skipper | Port/Launch Site

Dive of Day 1 2 3 4 | Surface Int. : | Time in : out :

	Pressure				DIVE TIME	MAX DEPTH
Mix	In	Out	Used	Cyl. Size		
					mins	m/ft

Tissue Code: Pre   Post | Deco Stops .... mins .... m/ft ....mins........ m/ft

Open Circuit ☐ Semi-Closed ☐ Closed Circuit ☐ Comp/Tables ....

Weight ....kg/lbs   OK: Y / N   (Add/Remove ....)

Suit/Undersuit ....Gloves Y / N   Hood Y / N   Hot / Cold / OK

Water Speed Slack / Slow / Steady / Fast | Temp @ Depth

Sea State | Wind Speed | Temp @ Surface

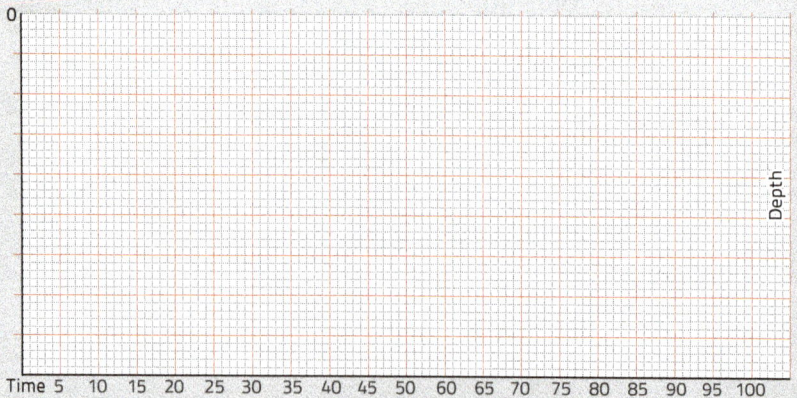

Time 5 10 15 20 25 30 35 40 45 50 55 60 65 70 75 80 85 90 95 100

Depth

Summary

Description/Sketch

Vis & Water Colour

m/ft

1
2
3
4
5
6
7
8
9
10
11
12
13
14
15
16
17
18
19
20
21
22
23
24
25

Accumulated Dive Time	Name	Verified by
:	Signature	
Milestone	No.	

DIVE LOG

DIVE No.

Date

Dive Site

Boat/Shore/Inland

Buddy

Purpose

Boat/Skipper

Port/Launch Site

Dive of Day   1   2   3   4   Surface Int.   :   Time in   :   out   :

| Mix | Pressure | | Used | Cyl. Size |
	In	Out		

DIVE TIME

mins

MAX DEPTH

m/ft

Tissue Code: Pre   Post   Deco Stops .... mins .... m/ft   .... mins .... m/ft

Open Circuit ☐   Semi-Closed ☐   Closed Circuit ☐   Comp/Tables ....

Weight ....kg/lbs   OK: Y / N   (Add/Remove ....)

Suit/Undersuit ....Gloves Y / N   Hood Y / N   Hot / Cold / OK

Water Speed   Slack / Slow / Steady / Fast   Temp @ Depth

Sea State   Wind Speed   Temp @ Surface

0

Depth

Time 5   10   15   20   25   30   35   40   45   50   55   60   65   70   75   80   85   90   95   100

Summary

Vis & Water Colour

m/ft

1
2
3
4
5
6
7
8
9
10
11
12
13
14
15
16
17
18
19
20
21
22
23
24
25

Description/Sketch

DIVED UP

Accumulated Dive Time		Verified by
:	Name	
Milestone	Signature	
	No.	

DIVE No.	**DIVE LOG**	Date

Dive Site   Boat/Shore/Inland

Buddy   Purpose

Boat/Skipper   Port/Launch Site

Dive of Day   1   2   3   4   Surface Int.   :   Time in   :   out   :

| Mix | Pressure | | Used | Cyl. Size | | |
	In	Out				

DIVE TIME   mins

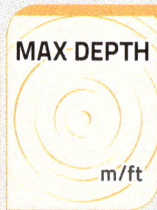

MAX DEPTH   m/ft

Tissue Code: Pre   Post   Deco Stops .... mins .... m/ft   ....mins........ m/ft

Open Circuit ☐   Semi-Closed ☐   Closed Circuit ☐   Comp/Tables ....

Weight ....kg/lbs   OK: Y / N   (Add/Remove ....)

Suit/Undersuit ....Gloves Y / N   Hood Y / N   Hot / Cold / OK

Water Speed   Slack / Slow / Steady / Fast   Temp @ Depth

Sea State   Wind Speed   Temp @ Surface

Time   5   10   15   20   25   30   35   40   45   50   55   60   65   70   75   80   85   90   95   100

Summary

Vis & Water Colour

m/ft

1
2
3
4
5
6
7
8
9
10
11
12
13
14
15
16
17
18
19
20
21
22
23
24
25

Description/Sketch

DIVED UP

Accumulated Dive Time

:

Milestone

Name

Signature

No.

Verified by

DIVE No.	**DIVE LOG**	Date

Dive Site   Boat/Shore/Inland

Buddy   Purpose

Boat/Skipper   Port/Launch Site

Dive of Day   1   2   3   4   Surface Int.   :   Time in   :   out   :

	Pressure				
Mix	In	Out	Used	Cyl. Size	

DIVE TIME   mins

MAX DEPTH   m/ft

Tissue Code: Pre   Post   Deco Stops .... mins .... m/ft   ....mins........ m/ft

Open Circuit ☐   Semi-Closed ☐   Closed Circuit ☐   Comp/Tables ....

Weight ....kg/lbs   OK: Y / N   (Add/Remove ....)

Suit/Undersuit ....Gloves Y / N   Hood Y / N   Hot / Cold / OK

Water Speed   Slack / Slow / Steady / Fast   Temp @ Depth

Sea State   Wind Speed   Temp @ Surface

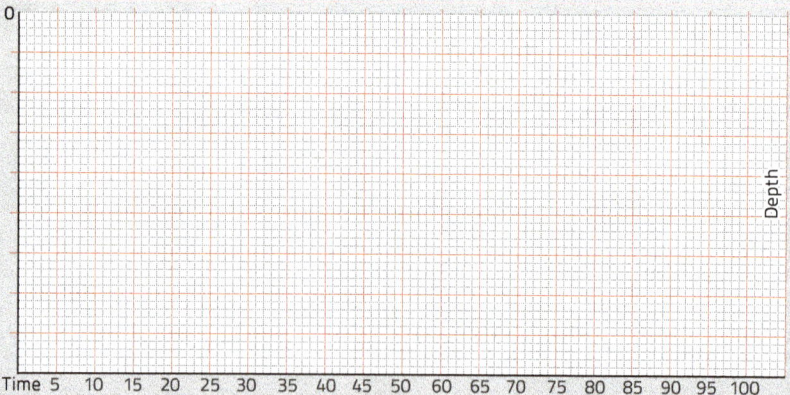

0

Depth

Time   5   10   15   20   25   30   35   40   45   50   55   60   65   70   75   80   85   90   95   100

Summary

Vis & Water Colour

m/ft

1
2
3
4
5
6
7
8
9
10
11
12
13
14
15
16
17
18
19
20
21
22
23
24
25

Description/Sketch

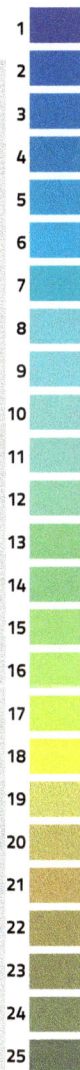

DIVED UP

Accumulated Dive Time	Name	
:	Signature	
Milestone	No.	Verified by

| DIVE No. | **DIVE LOG** | Date |

Dive Site | Boat/Shore/Inland

Buddy | Purpose

Boat/Skipper | Port/Launch Site

Dive of Day 1 2 3 4 | Surface Int. : | Time in : out :

Mix	Pressure		Used	Cyl. Size
	In	Out		

DIVE TIME .... mins

MAX DEPTH .... m/ft

Tissue Code: Pre   Post | Deco Stops .... mins .... m/ft .... mins .... m/ft

Open Circuit ☐   Semi-Closed ☐   Closed Circuit ☐   Comp/Tables ....

Weight .... kg/lbs   OK: Y / N   (Add/Remove ....)

Suit/Undersuit ....Gloves Y / N   Hood Y / N   Hot / Cold / OK

Water Speed Slack / Slow / Steady / Fast | Temp @ Depth

Sea State | Wind Speed | Temp @ Surface

0

Depth

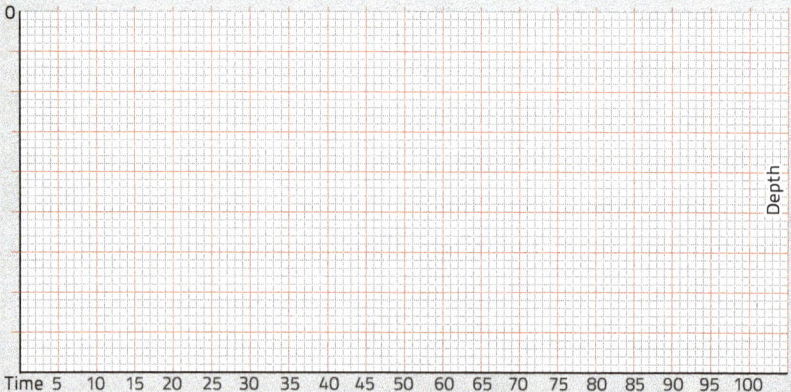

Time 5 10 15 20 25 30 35 40 45 50 55 60 65 70 75 80 85 90 95 100

Summary

Vis & Water Colour

m/ft

1
2
3
4
5
6
7
8
9
10
11
12
13
14
15
16
17
18
19
20
21
22
23
24
25

Description/Sketch

DIVED UP

Accumulated Dive Time	Name	Verified by
:	Signature	
Milestone	No.	

DIVE No.	**DIVE LOG**	Date

Dive Site | Boat/Shore/Inland

Buddy | Purpose

Boat/Skipper | Port/Launch Site

Dive of Day 1 2 3 4 | Surface Int.   : | Time in   :   out   :

	Pressure					
Mix	In	Out	Used	Cyl. Size	**DIVE TIME**	**MAX DEPTH**
					mins	m/ft

Tissue Code: Pre   Post | Deco Stops .... mins .... m/ft ....mins........m/ft

Open Circuit ☐   Semi-Closed ☐   Closed Circuit ☐   Comp/Tables ....

Weight ....kg/lbs   OK: Y / N   (Add/Remove ....)

Suit/Undersuit ....Gloves Y / N   Hood Y / N   Hot / Cold / OK

Water Speed Slack / Slow / Steady / Fast | Temp @ Depth

Sea State | Wind Speed | Temp @ Surface

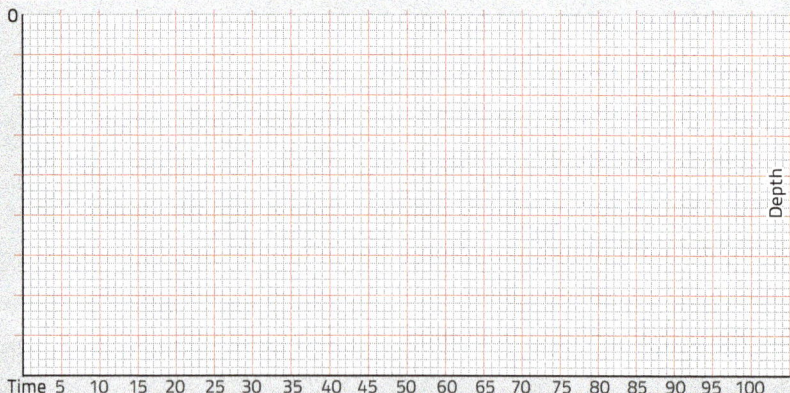

Time 5   10   15   20   25   30   35   40   45   50   55   60   65   70   75   80   85   90   95   100

Summary

Description/Sketch

Vis & Water Colour

m/ft

1
2
3
4
5
6
7
8
9
10
11
12
13
14
15
16
17
18
19
20
21
22
23
24
25

DIVED UP

Accumulated Dive Time		Verified by
:	Name	
Milestone	Signature	
	No.	

| DIVE No. | **DIVE LOG** | Date |

Dive Site
Boat/Shore/Inland

Buddy
Purpose

Boat/Skipper
Port/Launch Site

Dive of Day 1 2 3 4   Surface Int.   :   Time in   :   out   :

Mix	Pressure		Used	Cyl. Size
	In	Out		

DIVE TIME

mins

MAX DEPTH

m/ft

Tissue Code: Pre   Post   Deco Stops .... mins .... m/ft   ....mins .... m/ft

Open Circuit ☐ Semi-Closed ☐ Closed Circuit ☐ Comp/Tables ....

Weight ....kg/lbs   OK: Y / N   (Add/Remove ....)

Suit/Undersuit ....Gloves Y / N   Hood Y / N   Hot / Cold / OK

Water Speed Slack / Slow / Steady / Fast   Temp @ Depth

Sea State   Wind Speed   Temp @ Surface

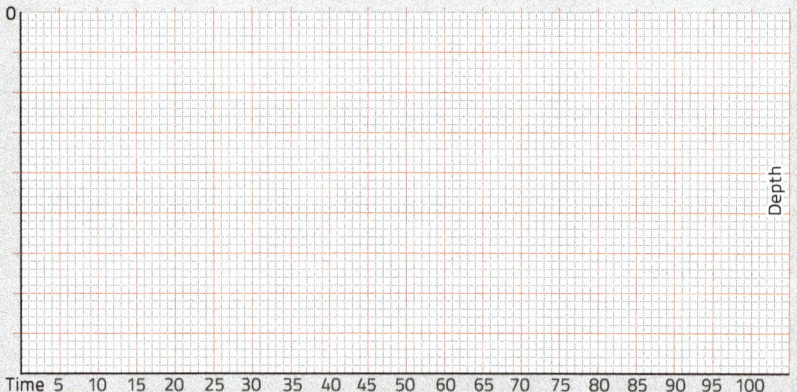

Summary

Description/Sketch

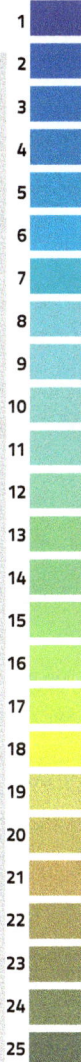

Vis & Water Colour

m/ft

1	
2	
3	
4	
5	
6	
7	
8	
9	
10	
11	
12	
13	
14	
15	
16	
17	
18	
19	
20	
21	
22	
23	
24	
25	

DIVED UP

Accumulated Dive Time

:

Milestone

Name

Signature

No.

Verified by

DIVE LOG

DIVE No.

Date

Dive Site   Boat/Shore/Inland

Buddy   Purpose

Boat/Skipper   Port/Launch Site

Dive of Day 1 2 3 4   Surface Int.   :   Time in   :   out   :

Mix	Pressure		Used	Cyl. Size
	In	Out		

DIVE TIME

mins

MAX DEPTH

m/ft

Tissue Code: Pre   Post   Deco Stops .... mins .... m/ft   .... mins .... m/ft

Open Circuit ☐ Semi-Closed ☐ Closed Circuit ☐ Comp/Tables ....

Weight .... kg/lbs   OK: Y / N   (Add/Remove ....)

Suit/Undersuit ....Gloves Y / N   Hood Y / N   Hot / Cold / OK

Water Speed Slack / Slow / Steady / Fast   Temp @ Depth

Sea State   Wind Speed   Temp @ Surface

Time 5 10 15 20 25 30 35 40 45 50 55 60 65 70 75 80 85 90 95 100

Depth

Summary

Vis & Water Colour

m/ft

1
2
3
4
5
6
7
8
9
10
11
12
13
14
15
16
17
18
19
20
21
22
23
24
25

Description/Sketch

DIVED UP

Accumulated Dive Time

:

Milestone

Name

Signature

No.

Verified by

DIVE No.   # DIVE LOG   **Date**

Dive Site   Boat/Shore/Inland

Buddy   Purpose

Boat/Skipper   Port/Launch Site

Dive of Day   1   2   3   4   Surface Int.   :   Time in   :   out   :

| | Pressure | | | | |
| Mix | In | Out | Used | Cyl. Size |

DIVE TIME

mins

MAX DEPTH

m/ft

Tissue Code: Pre   Post   Deco Stops .... mins .... m/ft .... mins .... m/ft

Open Circuit ☐   Semi-Closed ☐   Closed Circuit ☐   Comp/Tables ....

Weight .... kg/lbs   OK: Y / N   (Add/Remove ....)

Suit/Undersuit ....Gloves Y / N   Hood Y / N   Hot / Cold / OK

Water Speed   Slack / Slow / Steady / Fast   Temp @ Depth

Sea State   Wind Speed   Temp @ Surface

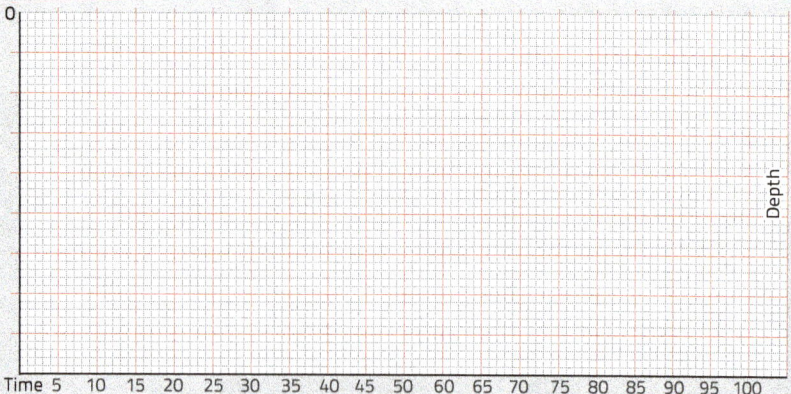

0

Depth

Time   5   10   15   20   25   30   35   40   45   50   55   60   65   70   75   80   85   90   95   100

Summary

Vis & Water Colour

m/ft

1
2
3
4
5
6
7
8
9
10
11
12
13
14
15
16
17
18
19
20
21
22
23
24
25

Description/Sketch

DIVED UP

Accumulated Dive Time

:

Milestone

Name

Signature

No.

Verified by

DIVE No.	DIVE LOG	Date

Dive Site   Boat/Shore/Inland

Buddy   Purpose

Boat/Skipper   Port/Launch Site

Dive of Day   1   2   3   4   Surface Int.   :   Time in   :   out   :

Mix	Pressure In	Pressure Out	Used	Cyl. Size

DIVE TIME   mins

MAX DEPTH   m/ft

Tissue Code: Pre   Post   Deco Stops .... mins .... m/ft .... mins .... m/ft

Open Circuit ☐   Semi-Closed ☐   Closed Circuit ☐   Comp/Tables ....

Weight ....kg/lbs   OK: Y / N   (Add/Remove ....)

Suit/Undersuit ....Gloves Y / N   Hood Y / N   Hot / Cold / OK

Water Speed   Slack / Slow / Steady / Fast   Temp @ Depth

Sea State   Wind Speed   Temp @ Surface

Time 5   10   15   20   25   30   35   40   45   50   55   60   65   70   75   80   85   90   95   100

Depth

Summary

Description/Sketch

1
2
3
4
5
6
7
8
9
10
11
12
13
14
15
16
17
18
19
20
21
22
23
24
25

DIVED UP

Accumulated Dive Time	Name	Verified by
:	Signature	
Milestone	No.	

DIVE No.	DIVE LOG	Date

Dive Site — Boat/Shore/Inland

Buddy — Purpose

Boat/Skipper — Port/Launch Site

Dive of Day   1   2   3   4   Surface Int.   :   Time in   :   out   :

Mix	Pressure In	Pressure Out	Used	Cyl. Size

DIVE TIME

mins

MAX DEPTH

m/ft

Tissue Code: Pre   Post   Deco Stops .... mins .... m/ft   ....mins ....m/ft

Open Circuit ☐   Semi-Closed ☐   Closed Circuit ☐   Comp/Tables ....

Weight ....kg/lbs   OK: Y / N   (Add/Remove ....)

Suit/Undersuit ....Gloves Y / N   Hood Y / N   Hot / Cold / OK

Water Speed   Slack / Slow / Steady / Fast   Temp @ Depth

Sea State   Wind Speed   Temp @ Surface

Time 5   10   15   20   25   30   35   40   45   50   55   60   65   70   75   80   85   90   95   100

Summary

Vis & Water Colour

m/ft

1
2
3
4
5
6
7
8
9
10
11
12
13
14
15
16
17
18
19
20
21
22
23
24
25

Description/Sketch

DIVED UP

Accumulated Dive Time

:

Milestone

Name

Signature

No.

Verified by

DIVE No.	DIVE LOG	Date

Dive Site   Boat/Shore/Inland

Buddy   Purpose

Boat/Skipper   Port/Launch Site

Dive of Day   1   2   3   4   Surface Int.   :   Time in   :   out   :

	Pressure					
Mix	In	Out	Used	Cyl. Size	DIVE TIME	MAX DEPTH
					mins	m/ft

Tissue Code: Pre   Post   Deco Stops .... mins .... m/ft   .... mins .... m/ft

Open Circuit ☐   Semi-Closed ☐   Closed Circuit ☐   Comp/Tables ....
Weight ....kg/lbs   OK: Y / N   (Add/Remove ....)
Suit/Undersuit ....Gloves Y / N   Hood Y / N   Hot / Cold / OK

Water Speed   Slack / Slow / Steady / Fast   Temp @ Depth
Sea State   Wind Speed   Temp @ Surface

0

Depth

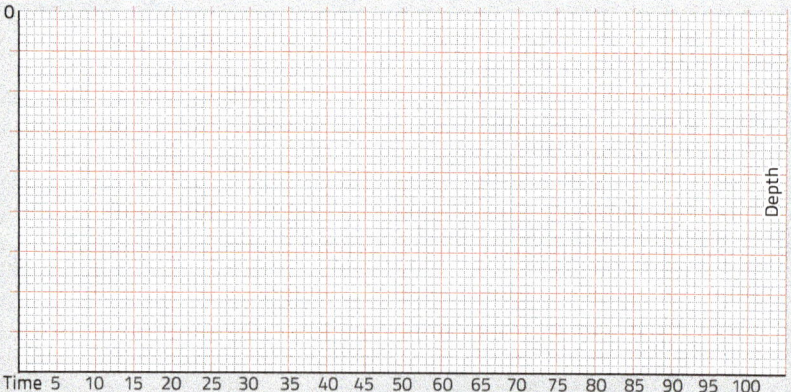

Time 5   10   15   20   25   30   35   40   45   50   55   60   65   70   75   80   85   90   95   100

Summary

Vis & Water Colour

m/ft 1
2
3
4
5
6
7
8
9
10
11
12
13
14
15
16
17
18
19
20
21
22
23
24
25

Description/Sketch

DIVED UP

Accumulated Dive Time
:

Milestone

Name

Signature

No.

Verified by

DIVE No.	DIVE LOG	Date

Dive Site   Boat/Shore/Inland

Buddy   Purpose

Boat/Skipper   Port/Launch Site

Dive of Day 1 2 3 4   Surface Int.   :   Time in   :   out   :

	Pressure					
Mix	In	Out	Used	Cyl. Size		

DIVE TIME   **MAX DEPTH**

mins   m/ft

Tissue Code: Pre   Post   Deco Stops .... mins .... m/ft .... mins .... m/ft

Open Circuit ☐   Semi-Closed ☐   Closed Circuit ☐   Comp/Tables ....

Weight .... kg/lbs   OK: Y / N   (Add/Remove ....)

Suit/Undersuit ....Gloves Y / N   Hood Y / N   Hot / Cold / OK

Water Speed Slack / Slow / Steady / Fast   Temp @ Depth

Sea State   Wind Speed   Temp @ Surface

0

Depth

Time 5 10 15 20 25 30 35 40 45 50 55 60 65 70 75 80 85 90 95 100

Summary

Vis & Water Colour

m/ft

Description/Sketch

1
2
3
4
5
6
7
8
9
10
11
12
13
14
15
16
17
18
19
20
21
22
23
24
25

DIVED UP

Accumulated Dive Time

:

Milestone

Name

Signature

No.

Verified by

DIVE LOG

DIVE No.

Date

Dive Site

Boat/Shore/Inland

Buddy

Purpose

Boat/Skipper

Port/Launch Site

Dive of Day 1 2 3 4   Surface Int.   :   Time in   :   out   :

Mix	Pressure		Used	Cyl. Size
	In	Out		

DIVE TIME

mins

MAX DEPTH

m/ft

Tissue Code: Pre   Post   Deco Stops .... mins .... m/ft ....mins........ m/ft

Open Circuit ☐   Semi-Closed ☐   Closed Circuit ☐   Comp/Tables ....

Weight ....kg/lbs   OK: Y / N   (Add/Remove ....)

Suit/Undersuit ....Gloves Y / N   Hood Y / N   Hot / Cold / OK

Water Speed Slack / Slow / Steady / Fast   Temp @ Depth

Sea State   Wind Speed   Temp @ Surface

0

Depth

Time 5 10 15 20 25 30 35 40 45 50 55 60 65 70 75 80 85 90 95 100

Summary

Vis & Water Colour

m/ft

1	
2	
3	
4	
5	
6	
7	
8	
9	
10	
11	
12	
13	
14	
15	
16	
17	
18	
19	
20	
21	
22	
23	
24	
25	

Description/Sketch

DIVED UP

Accumulated Dive Time

:

Milestone

Name

Signature

No.

Verified by

DIVE LOG

DIVE No.	DIVE LOG	Date

Dive Site   Boat/Shore/Inland

Buddy   Purpose

Boat/Skipper   Port/Launch Site

Dive of Day   1   2   3   4   Surface Int.   :   Time in   :   out   :

	Pressure				DIVE TIME	MAX DEPTH
Mix	In	Out	Used	Cyl. Size		
					mins	m/ft

Tissue Code: Pre   Post   Deco Stops .... mins .... m/ft ....mins .... m/ft

Open Circuit ☐   Semi-Closed ☐   Closed Circuit ☐   Comp/Tables ....

Weight ....kg/lbs   OK: Y / N   (Add/Remove ....)

Suit/Undersuit ....Gloves Y / N   Hood Y / N   Hot / Cold / OK

Water Speed   Slack / Slow / Steady / Fast   Temp @ Depth

Sea State   Wind Speed   Temp @ Surface

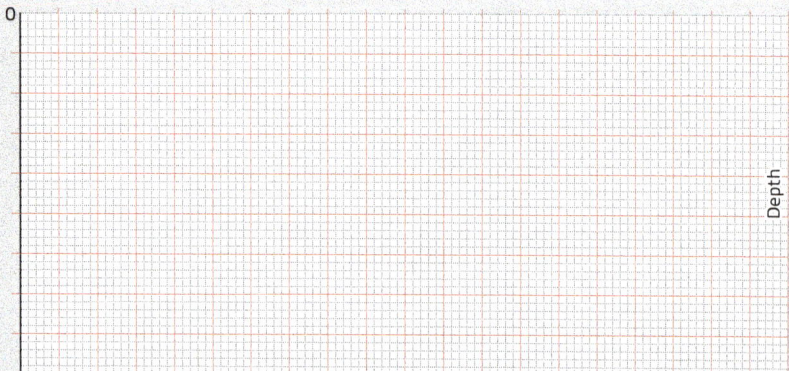

Time   5   10   15   20   25   30   35   40   45   50   55   60   65   70   75   80   85   90   95   100

Depth

Summary

Vis & Water Colour

m/ft

1
2
3
4
5
6
7
8
9
10
11
12
13
14
15
16
17
18
19
20
21
22
23
24
25

Description/Sketch

DIVED UP

Accumulated Dive Time

:

Milestone

Name

Signature

No.

Verified by

DIVE LOG

DIVE No.

Date

Dive Site

Boat/Shore/Inland

Buddy

Purpose

Boat/Skipper

Port/Launch Site

Dive of Day   1   2   3   4   Surface Int.   :   Time in   :   out   :

| Mix | Pressure | | Used | Cyl. Size |
	In	Out		

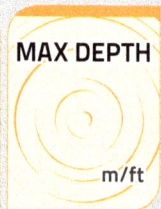

DIVE TIME

mins

MAX DEPTH

m/ft

Tissue Code: Pre   Post   Deco Stops .... mins .... m/ft   .... mins .... m/ft

Open Circuit ☐   Semi-Closed ☐   Closed Circuit ☐   Comp/Tables ....

Weight .... kg/lbs   OK: Y / N   (Add/Remove ....)

Suit/Undersuit ....Gloves Y / N   Hood Y / N   Hot / Cold / OK

Water Speed Slack / Slow / Steady / Fast   Temp @ Depth

Sea State   Wind Speed   Temp @ Surface

Time 5   10   15   20   25   30   35   40   45   50   55   60   65   70   75   80   85   90   95   100

Depth

Summary

Vis & Water Colour

m/ft

1
2
3
4
5
6
7
8
9
10
11
12
13
14
15
16
17
18
19
20
21
22
23
24
25

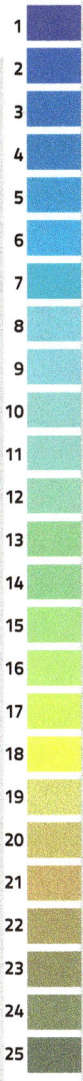

Description/Sketch

DIVED UP

Accumulated Dive Time

:

Milestone

Name

Signature

No.

Verified by

DIVE No.	DIVE LOG	Date

Dive Site   Boat/Shore/Inland

Buddy   Purpose

Boat/Skipper   Port/Launch Site

Dive of Day   1   2   3   4   Surface Int.   :   Time in   :   out   :

Mix	Pressure		Used	Cyl. Size
	In	Out		

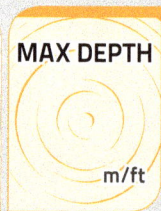

DIVE TIME   mins

MAX DEPTH   m/ft

Tissue Code: Pre   Post   Deco Stops .... mins .... m/ft ....mins........ m/ft

Open Circuit ☐   Semi-Closed ☐   Closed Circuit ☐   Comp/Tables ....

Weight ....kg/lbs   OK: Y / N   (Add/Remove ....)

Suit/Undersuit ....Gloves Y / N   Hood Y / N   Hot / Cold / OK

Water Speed   Slack / Slow / Steady / Fast   Temp @ Depth

Sea State   Wind Speed   Temp @ Surface

0

Depth

Time   5   10   15   20   25   30   35   40   45   50   55   60   65   70   75   80   85   90   95   100

Summary

m/ft

1
2
3
4
5
6
7
8
9
10
11
12
13
14
15
16
17
18
19
20
21
22
23
24
25

Description/Sketch

DIVED UP

Accumulated Dive Time

:

Milestone

Name

Signature

No.

Verified by

DIVE No.

DIVE LOG

Date

Dive Site   Boat/Shore/Inland

Buddy   Purpose

Boat/Skipper   Port/Launch Site

Dive of Day 1 2 3 4   Surface Int.   :   Time in   :   out   :

	Pressure			
Mix	In	Out	Used	Cyl. Size

DIVE TIME

mins

MAX DEPTH

m/ft

Tissue Code: Pre   Post   Deco Stops .... mins .... m/ft   .... mins .... m/ft

Open Circuit ☐   Semi-Closed ☐   Closed Circuit ☐   Comp/Tables ....
Weight .... kg/lbs   OK: Y / N   (Add/Remove ....)
Suit/Undersuit .... Gloves Y / N   Hood Y / N   Hot / Cold / OK

Water Speed   Slack / Slow / Steady / Fast   Temp @ Depth
Sea State   Wind Speed   Temp @ Surface

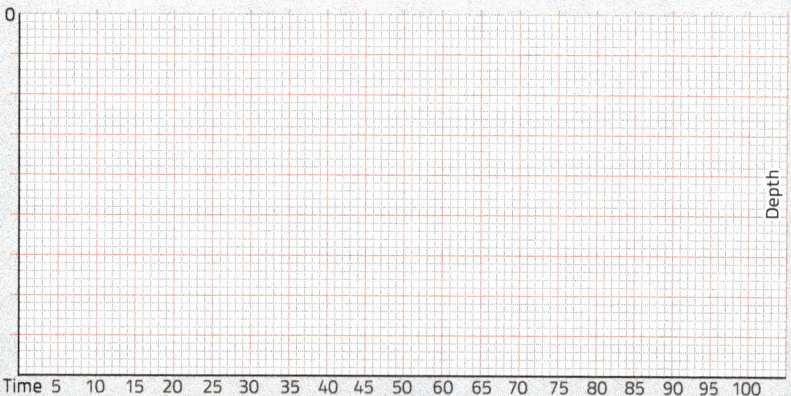

Summary

Description/Sketch

Vis & Water Colour

m/ft

1
2
3
4
5
6
7
8
9
10
11
12
13
14
15
16
17
18
19
20
21
22
23
24
25

Accumulated Dive Time

:

Milestone

Name

Signature

No.

Verified by

DIVE No.	**DIVE LOG**	Date

Dive Site   Boat/Shore/Inland

Buddy   Purpose

Boat/Skipper   Port/Launch Site

Dive of Day   1   2   3   4   Surface Int.   :   Time in   :   out   :

	Pressure				
Mix	In	Out	Used	Cyl. Size	

DIVE TIME

mins

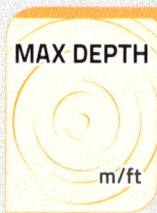

MAX DEPTH

m/ft

Tissue Code: Pre   Post   Deco Stops .... mins .... m/ft   ....mins........ m/ft

Open Circuit ☐   Semi-Closed ☐   Closed Circuit ☐   Comp/Tables ....

Weight ....kg/lbs   OK: Y / N   (Add/Remove ....)

Suit/Undersuit ....Gloves Y / N   Hood Y / N   Hot / Cold / OK

Water Speed   Slack / Slow / Steady / Fast   Temp @ Depth

Sea State   Wind Speed   Temp @ Surface

Summary

Vis & Water Colour

m/ft

1
2
3
4
5
6
7
8
9
10
11
12
13
14
15
16
17
18
19
20
21
22
23
24
25

Description/Sketch

DIVED UP

Accumulated Dive Time

:

Milestone

Name

Signature

No.

Verified by

DIVE LOG

DIVE No.

Date

Dive Site

Boat/Shore/Inland

Buddy

Purpose

Boat/Skipper

Port/Launch Site

Dive of Day 1 2 3 4   Surface Int.   :   Time in   :   out   :

Mix	Pressure		Used	Cyl. Size
	In	Out		

DIVE TIME

mins

MAX DEPTH

m/ft

Tissue Code: Pre   Post   Deco Stops .... mins .... m/ft   .... mins .... m/ft

Open Circuit ☐   Semi-Closed ☐   Closed Circuit ☐   Comp/Tables ....

Weight ....kg/lbs   OK: Y / N   (Add/Remove ....)

Suit/Undersuit ....Gloves Y / N   Hood Y / N   Hot / Cold / OK

Water Speed   Slack / Slow / Steady / Fast   Temp @ Depth

Sea State   Wind Speed   Temp @ Surface

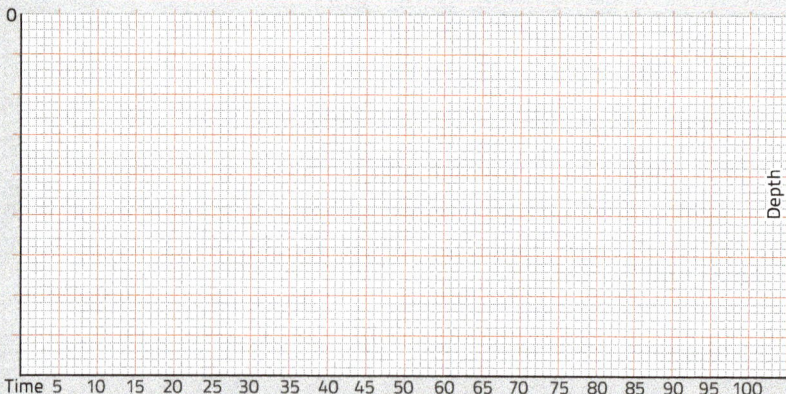

Time 5   10   15   20   25   30   35   40   45   50   55   60   65   70   75   80   85   90   95 100

Depth

Summary

Description/Sketch

Vis & Water Colour

m/ft

1
2
3
4
5
6
7
8
9
10
11
12
13
14
15
16
17
18
19
20
21
22
23
24
25

DIVED UP

Accumulated Dive Time

:

Milestone

Name

Signature

No.

Verified by

DIVE LOG

DIVE No.

Date

Dive Site   Boat/Shore/Inland

Buddy   Purpose

Boat/Skipper   Port/Launch Site

Dive of Day   1   2   3   4   Surface Int.   :   Time in   :   out   :

Mix	Pressure		Used	Cyl. Size
	In	Out		

DIVE TIME   **MAX DEPTH**

mins   m/ft

Tissue Code: Pre   Post   Deco Stops .... mins .... m/ft .... mins .... m/ft

Open Circuit ☐   Semi-Closed ☐   Closed Circuit ☐   Comp/Tables ....

Weight ....kg/lbs   OK: Y / N   (Add/Remove ....)

Suit/Undersuit ....Gloves Y / N   Hood Y / N   Hot / Cold / OK

Water Speed   Slack / Slow / Steady / Fast   Temp @ Depth

Sea State   Wind Speed   Temp @ Surface

Depth

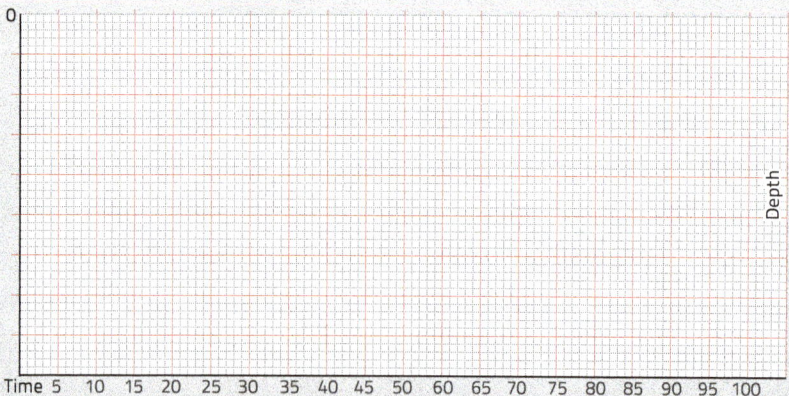

Time 5   10   15   20   25   30   35   40   45   50   55   60   65   70   75   80   85   90   95   100

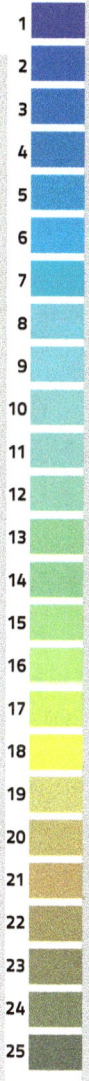

Summary

Description/Sketch

Vis & Water Colour

m/ft

1
2
3
4
5
6
7
8
9
10
11
12
13
14
15
16
17
18
19
20
21
22
23
24
25

DIVED UP

Accumulated Dive Time	Name	Verified by
:	Signature	
Milestone	No.	

Dive Site	Boat/Shore/Inland

Buddy	Purpose

Boat/Skipper	Port/Launch Site

Dive of Day   1   2   3   4   Surface Int.   :   Time in   :   out   :

	Pressure			
Mix	In	Out	Used	Cyl. Size

DIVE TIME

mins

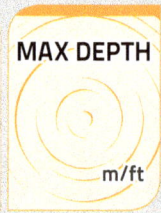

MAX DEPTH

m/ft

Tissue Code: Pre   Post   Deco Stops .... mins .... m/ft   .... mins .... m/ft

Open Circuit ☐   Semi-Closed ☐   Closed Circuit ☐   Comp/Tables ....

Weight ....kg/lbs   OK: Y / N   (Add/Remove ....)

Suit/Undersuit ....Gloves Y / N   Hood Y / N   Hot / Cold / OK

Water Speed   Slack / Slow / Steady / Fast   Temp @ Depth

Sea State   Wind Speed   Temp @ Surface

Summary

Description/Sketch

Vis & Water Colour

m/ft

1	
2	
3	
4	
5	
6	
7	
8	
9	
10	
11	
12	
13	
14	
15	
16	
17	
18	
19	
20	
21	
22	
23	
24	
25	

Accumulated Dive Time

:

Milestone

Name

Signature

No.

Verified by

DIVE LOG

DIVE No.	DIVE LOG	Date

Dive Site   Boat/Shore/Inland

Buddy   Purpose

Boat/Skipper   Port/Launch Site

Dive of Day   1   2   3   4   Surface Int.   :   Time in   :   out   :

		Pressure				
Mix	In	Out	Used	Cyl. Size		

DIVE TIME   mins

MAX DEPTH   m/ft

Tissue Code: Pre   Post   Deco Stops .... mins ...... m/ft ....mins....... m/ft

Open Circuit ☐   Semi-Closed ☐   Closed Circuit ☐   Comp/Tables ....

Weight ....kg/lbs   OK: Y / N   (Add/Remove ....)

Suit/Undersuit ....Gloves Y / N   Hood Y / N   Hot / Cold / OK

Water Speed   Slack / Slow / Steady / Fast   Temp @ Depth

Sea State   Wind Speed   Temp @ Surface

0   Depth

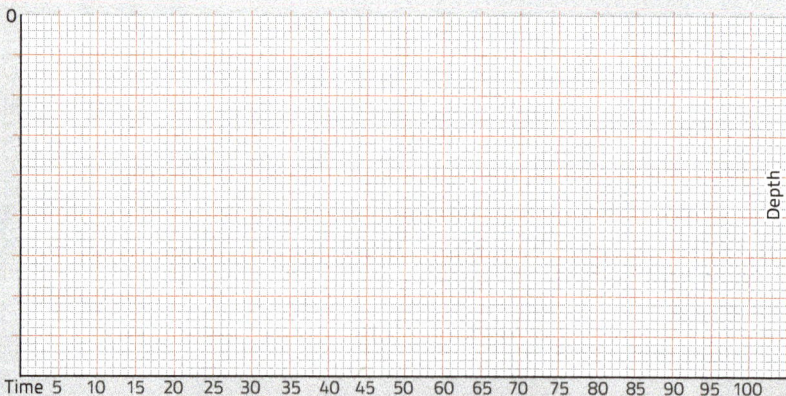

Time 5   10   15   20   25   30   35   40   45   50   55   60   65   70   75   80   85   90   95   100

Summary

Vis & Water Colour

m/ft

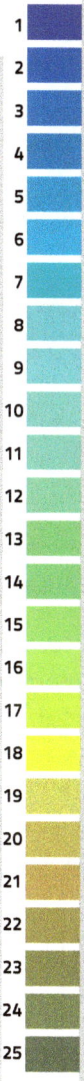

Description/Sketch

| 1 |
| 2 |
| 3 |
| 4 |
| 5 |
| 6 |
| 7 |
| 8 |
| 9 |
| 10 |
| 11 |
| 12 |
| 13 |
| 14 |
| 15 |
| 16 |
| 17 |
| 18 |
| 19 |
| 20 |
| 21 |
| 22 |
| 23 |
| 24 |
| 25 |

DIVED UP

Accumulated Dive Time

:

Milestone

Name

Signature

No.

Verified by

DIVE No.	**DIVE LOG**	Date

Dive Site   Boat/Shore/Inland

Buddy   Purpose

Boat/Skipper   Port/Launch Site

Dive of Day   1   2   3   4   Surface Int.   :   Time in   :   out   :

		Pressure				
Mix	In	Out	Used	Cyl. Size

DIVE TIME

mins

MAX DEPTH

m/ft

Tissue Code: Pre   Post   Deco Stops .... mins .... m/ft   .... mins .... m/ft

Open Circuit ☐   Semi-Closed ☐   Closed Circuit ☐   Comp/Tables ....

Weight ....kg/lbs   OK: Y / N   (Add/Remove ....)

Suit/Undersuit ....Gloves Y / N   Hood Y / N   Hot / Cold / OK

Water Speed   Slack / Slow / Steady / Fast   Temp @ Depth

Sea State   Wind Speed   Temp @ Surface

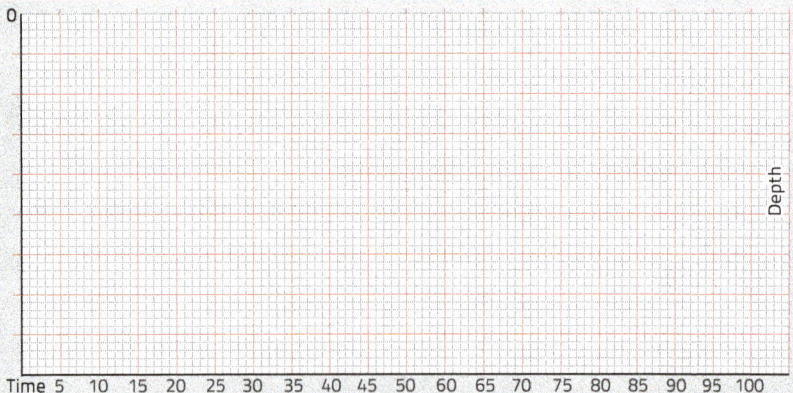

Time   5   10   15   20   25   30   35   40   45   50   55   60   65   70   75   80   85   90   95   100

Summary

Description/Sketch

Vis & Water Colour

m/ft

1
2
3
4
5
6
7
8
9
10
11
12
13
14
15
16
17
18
19
20
21
22
23
24
25

Accumulated Dive Time

:

Milestone

Name

Signature

No.

Verified by

DIVE No.	**DIVE LOG**	Date

Dive Site   Boat/Shore/Inland

Buddy   Purpose

Boat/Skipper   Port/Launch Site

Dive of Day   1   2   3   4   Surface Int.   :   Time in   :   out   :

	Pressure					
Mix	In	Out	Used	Cyl. Size		

DIVE TIME   mins

MAX DEPTH   m/ft

Tissue Code: Pre   Post   Deco Stops .... mins .... m/ft ....mins........ m/ft

Open Circuit ☐   Semi-Closed ☐   Closed Circuit ☐   Comp/Tables ....

Weight ....kg/lbs   OK: Y / N   (Add/Remove ....)

Suit/Undersuit ....Gloves Y / N   Hood Y / N   Hot / Cold / OK

Water Speed   Slack / Slow / Steady / Fast   Temp @ Depth

Sea State   Wind Speed   Temp @ Surface

Time   5   10   15   20   25   30   35   40   45   50   55   60   65   70   75   80   85   90   95   100

Summary

Vis & Water Colour

m/ft

1	
2	
3	
4	
5	
6	
7	
8	
9	
10	
11	
12	
13	
14	
15	
16	
17	
18	
19	
20	
21	
22	
23	
24	
25	

Description/Sketch

DIVED UP

Accumulated Dive Time

:

Milestone

Name

Signature

No.

Verified by

DIVE LOG

DIVE No.

Date

Dive Site   Boat/Shore/Inland

Buddy   Purpose

Boat/Skipper   Port/Launch Site

Dive of Day   1   2   3   4   Surface Int.   :   Time in   :   out   :

Mix	Pressure In	Out	Used	Cyl. Size	DIVE TIME	MAX DEPTH
					mins	m/ft

Tissue Code: Pre   Post   Deco Stops .... mins .... m/ft ....mins........ m/ft

Open Circuit ☐   Semi-Closed ☐   Closed Circuit ☐   Comp/Tables ....
Weight ....kg/lbs   OK: Y / N   (Add/Remove ....)
Suit/Undersuit ....Gloves Y / N   Hood Y / N   Hot / Cold / OK

Water Speed   Slack / Slow / Steady / Fast   Temp @ Depth
Sea State   Wind Speed   Temp @ Surface

0

Depth

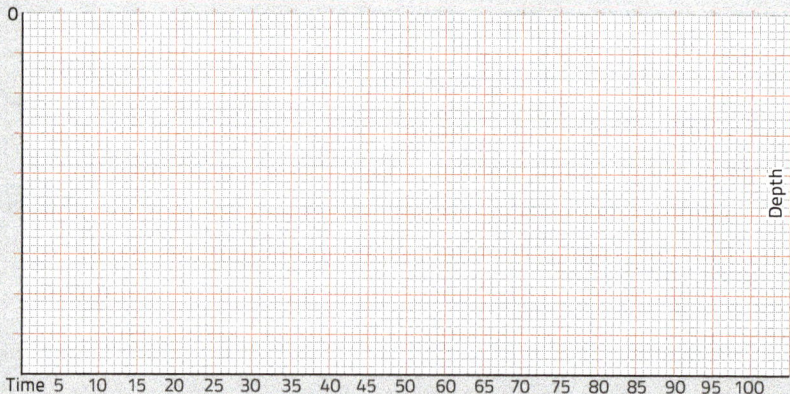

Time 5   10   15   20   25   30   35   40   45   50   55   60   65   70   75   80   85   90   95   100

Summary

Description/Sketch

m/ft

1
2
3
4
5
6
7
8
9
10
11
12
13
14
15
16
17
18
19
20
21
22
23
24
25

DIVED UP

Accumulated Dive Time

:

Milestone

Name

Signature

No.

Verified by

DIVE No.	**DIVE LOG**	Date

Dive Site Boat/Shore/Inland

Buddy Purpose

Boat/Skipper Port/Launch Site

Dive of Day 1 2 3 4   Surface Int. :   Time in :   out :

Mix	Pressure		Used	Cyl. Size
	In	Out		

DIVE TIME mins

MAX DEPTH m/ft

Tissue Code: Pre   Post   Deco Stops .... mins .... m/ft ....mins........ m/ft

Open Circuit ☐ Semi-Closed ☐ Closed Circuit ☐ Comp/Tables ....

Weight ....kg/lbs   OK: Y / N   (Add/Remove ....)

Suit/Undersuit ....Gloves Y / N   Hood Y / N   Hot / Cold / OK

Water Speed Slack / Slow / Steady / Fast   Temp @ Depth

Sea State   Wind Speed   Temp @ Surface

0

Depth

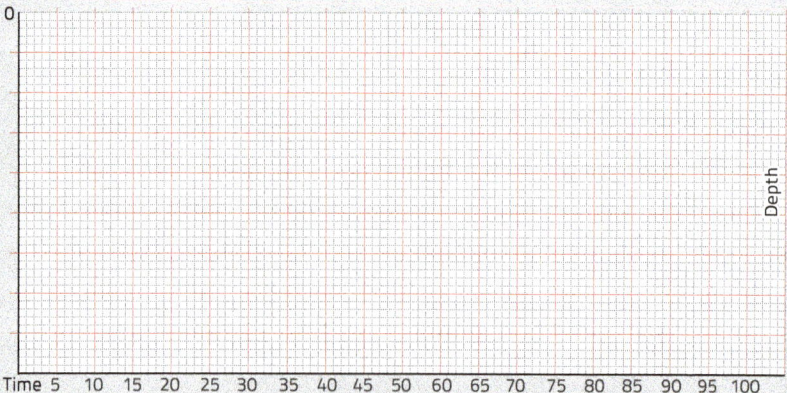

Time 5 10 15 20 25 30 35 40 45 50 60 65 70 75 80 85 90 95 100

Summary

Description/Sketch

Vis & Water Colour

m/ft

1
2
3
4
5
6
7
8
9
10
11
12
13
14
15
16
17
18
19
20
21
22
23
24
25

DIVED UP

Accumulated Dive Time

:

Milestone

Name

Signature

No.

Verified by

| DIVE No. | DIVE LOG | Date |

Dive Site   Boat/Shore/Inland

Buddy   Purpose

Boat/Skipper   Port/Launch Site

Dive of Day   1   2   3   4   Surface Int.   :   Time in   :   out   :

Mix	Pressure		Used	Cyl. Size
	In	Out		

DIVE TIME

mins

MAX DEPTH

m/ft

Tissue Code: Pre   Post   Deco Stops .... mins .... m/ft   ....mins........ m/ft

Open Circuit ☐   Semi-Closed ☐   Closed Circuit ☐   Comp/Tables ....

Weight ....kg/lbs   OK: Y / N   (Add/Remove ....)

Suit/Undersuit ....Gloves Y / N   Hood Y / N   Hot / Cold / OK

Water Speed   Slack / Slow / Steady / Fast   Temp @ Depth

Sea State   Wind Speed   Temp @ Surface

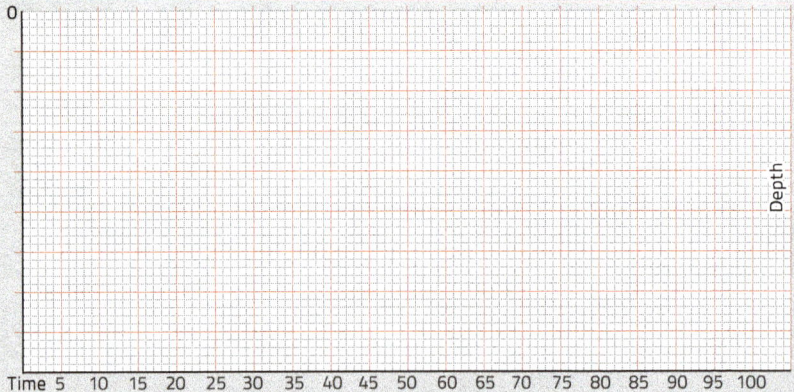

Time   5   10   15   20   25   30   35   40   45   50   55   60   65   70   75   80   85   90   95   100

Summary

Vis & Water Colour

m/ft

1	
2	
3	
4	
5	
6	
7	
8	
9	
10	
11	
12	
13	
14	
15	
16	
17	
18	
19	
20	
21	
22	
23	
24	
25	

Description/Sketch

DIVED UP

Accumulated Dive Time

:

Milestone

Name

Signature

No.

Verified by

DIVE No.	DIVE LOG	Date

Dive Site   Boat/Shore/Inland

Buddy   Purpose

Boat/Skipper   Port/Launch Site

Dive of Day 1 2 3 4   Surface Int.   :   Time in   :   out   :

	Pressure					
Mix	In	Out	Used	Cyl. Size	**DIVE TIME**  mins	**MAX DEPTH**  m/ft

Tissue Code: Pre   Post   Deco Stops .... mins .... m/ft .... mins .... m/ft

Open Circuit ☐   Semi-Closed ☐   Closed Circuit ☐   Comp/Tables ....
Weight .... kg/lbs   OK: Y / N   (Add/Remove ....)
Suit/Undersuit .... Gloves Y / N   Hood Y / N   Hot / Cold / OK

Water Speed Slack / Slow / Steady / Fast   Temp @ Depth
Sea State   Wind Speed   Temp @ Surface

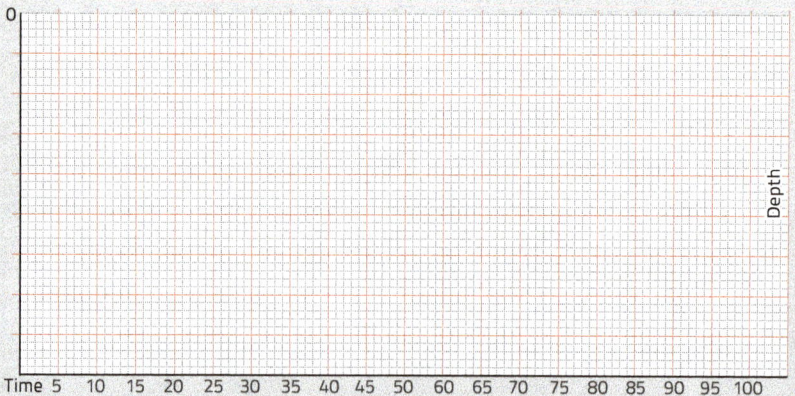

Summary

Vis & Water Colour

m/ft

1
2
3
4
5
6
7
8
9
10
11
12
13
14
15
16
17
18
19
20
21
22
23
24
25

Description/Sketch

DIVED UP

Accumulated Dive Time

:

Milestone

Name

Signature

No.

Verified by

DIVE No.	**DIVE LOG**	Date

Dive Site — Boat/Shore/Inland

Buddy — Purpose

Boat/Skipper — Port/Launch Site

Dive of Day 1 2 3 4   Surface Int. :   Time in :   out :

		Pressure			**DIVE TIME**	**MAX DEPTH**
Mix	In	Out	Used	Cyl. Size		
					mins	m/ft

Tissue Code: Pre   Post   Deco Stops .... mins .... m/ft .... mins .... m/ft

Open Circuit ☐   Semi-Closed ☐   Closed Circuit ☐   Comp/Tables ....
Weight .... kg/lbs   OK: Y / N   (Add/Remove ....)
Suit/Undersuit ....Gloves Y / N   Hood Y / N   Hot / Cold / OK

Water Speed   Slack / Slow / Steady / Fast   Temp @ Depth
Sea State   Wind Speed   Temp @ Surface

0

Depth

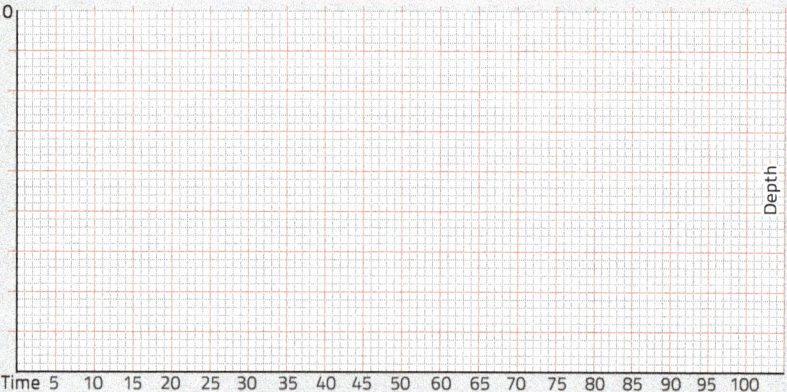

Time 5   10   15   20   25   30   35   40   45   50   60   65   70   75   80   85   90   95   100

Summary

Vis & Water Colour

m/ft

Description/Sketch

1
2
3
4
5
6
7
8
9
10
11
12
13
14
15
16
17
18
19
20
21
22
23
24
25

DIVED UP

Accumulated Dive Time

:

Milestone

Name

Signature

No.

Verified by

DIVE LOG

DIVE No.		Date

Dive Site   Boat/Shore/Inland

Buddy   Purpose

Boat/Skipper   Port/Launch Site

Dive of Day   1   2   3   4   Surface Int.   :   Time in   :   out   :

		Pressure			DIVE TIME	MAX DEPTH
Mix	In	Out	Used	Cyl. Size		

DIVE TIME   mins

MAX DEPTH   m/ft

Tissue Code: Pre   Post   Deco Stops .... mins .... m/ft .... mins .... m/ft

Open Circuit ☐   Semi-Closed ☐   Closed Circuit ☐   Comp/Tables ....

Weight ....kg/lbs   OK: Y / N   (Add/Remove ....)

Suit/Undersuit ....Gloves Y / N   Hood Y / N   Hot / Cold / OK

Water Speed   Slack / Slow / Steady / Fast   Temp @ Depth

Sea State   Wind Speed   Temp @ Surface

0

Depth

Time   5   10   15   20   25   30   35   40   45   50   55   60   65   70   75   80   85   90   95   100

Summary

Vis & Water Colour

m/ft

1	
2	
3	
4	
5	
6	
7	
8	
9	
10	
11	
12	
13	
14	
15	
16	
17	
18	
19	
20	
21	
22	
23	
24	
25	

Description/Sketch

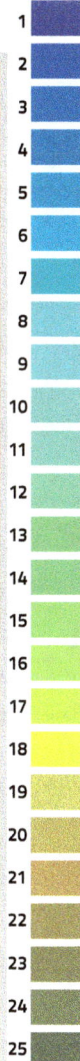

DIVED UP

Accumulated Dive Time		
:	Name	Verified by
Milestone	Signature	
	No.	

DIVE No.	DIVE LOG	Date

Dive Site   Boat/Shore/Inland

Buddy   Purpose

Boat/Skipper   Port/Launch Site

Dive of Day   1   2   3   4 | Surface Int.   : | Time in   :   out   :

	Pressure			
Mix	In	Out	Used	Cyl. Size

DIVE TIME
mins

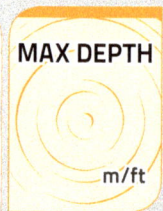

MAX DEPTH
m/ft

Tissue Code: Pre   Post | Deco Stops .... mins .... m/ft   ....mins........ m/ft

Open Circuit ☐   Semi-Closed ☐   Closed Circuit ☐   Comp/Tables ....

Weight ....kg/lbs   OK: Y / N   (Add/Remove ....)

Suit/Undersuit ....Gloves Y / N   Hood Y / N   Hot / Cold / OK

Water Speed   Slack / Slow / Steady / Fast   Temp @ Depth

Sea State   Wind Speed   Temp @ Surface

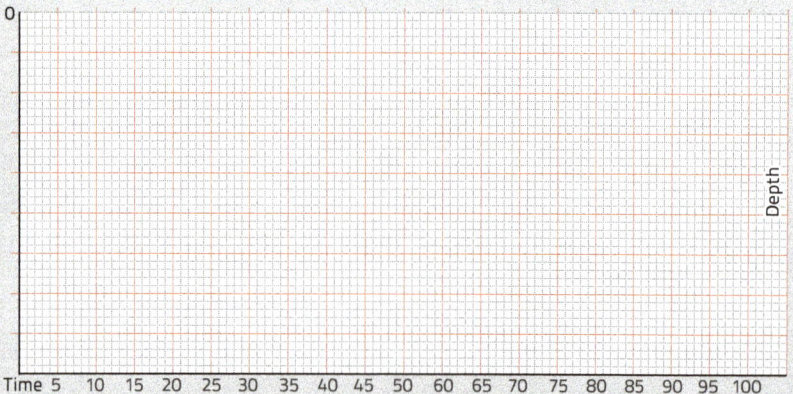

Summary

Vis & Water Colour

m/ft

1	
2	
3	
4	
5	
6	
7	
8	
9	
10	
11	
12	
13	
14	
15	
16	
17	
18	
19	
20	
21	
22	
23	
24	
25	

Description/Sketch

DIVED UP

Accumulated Dive Time

:

Milestone

Name

Signature

No.

Verified by

Winning Images with ANY Underwater Camera

The Essential Guide to Creating Engaging Photos

by Paul Colley, with a Foreword by Alex Mustard

'For all underwater photographers who want to
get ahead of the game': *UWP Magazine*

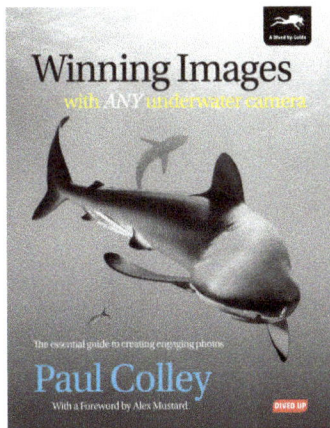

'Excellently written, highly informative and well-executed…
the essential guide on this subject': *Diver magazine*

'Will arm and inspire you to transform your underwater
photographs, whatever camera you use': Alex Mustard

- Learn how to take photos like the pros
- Secrets of great composition revealed
- One book, any camera

2014 | Paperback and Ebook | ISBN 978-1-909455-04-7

For more details and to order go to **DivedUp.com**

www.ingramcontent.com/pod-product-compliance
Lightning Source LLC
Chambersburg PA
CBHW052133090426
42741CB00009B/2070